FLOWERS DO SPEAK

FLOWERS DO SPEAK

... And a Black Flower Told Me ...

AFRODITE STATHI

RESOURCE *Publications* • Eugene, Oregon

FLOWERS DO SPEAK
. . . And a Black Flower Told Me . . .

Copyright © 2022 Afrodite Stathi. All rights reserved. Except for brief quotations in critical publications or reviews, no part of this book may be reproduced in any manner without prior written permission from the publisher. Write: Permissions, Wipf and Stock Publishers, 199 W. 8th Ave., Suite 3, Eugene, OR 97401.

Resource Publications
An Imprint of Wipf and Stock Publishers
199 W. 8th Ave., Suite 3
Eugene, OR 97401

www.wipfandstock.com

PAPERBACK ISBN: 978-1-6667-5466-7
HARDCOVER ISBN: 978-1-6667-5467-4
EBOOK ISBN: 978-1-6667-5468-1

08/29/22

CONTENTS

DOING TIME | 1
DEATH SENTENCE | 2
FATHER | 3
NOTHING | 5
INVISIBLE CAGE | 6
IN VAIN | 7
CONFESSION | 8
NIGHT INSIDE | 9
SO ALIKE | 10
INSIDE | 11
DARLING | 12
HEART | 13
LONELY | 14
EAGLE | 15
BLIND | 16
THE AFFAIR | 17
BEST FRIEND | 18
I PRAY | 19
TV or NOT TV. | 20
WHITE PAGE | 21
CYPRESS | 22
LIFE | 23
MULTIPLE CHOICES | 24
A WALK | 25
INVISIBLE | 26
FREE BIRDS | 27
THE LIFE I HAD | 29
THE CAT | 30
CAGE | 31
SUCCESS STORY | 32
AT LAST | 33
THE YEAR | 34
CREMATION | 35
NET | 36
IRONY | 38
MY CASE | 39
THE CHANGE | 40
DIE | 41
SOLITUDE | 42
WE ARE | 43
HEAVY RAIN | 44
POETRY | 45
TEARS | 47
SAVE THE DATE | 48
HOUSEWIFE | 49
NEW YEAR, MY DEAR | 51
FOOL STOP | 52
SUN AND RAIN | 53
DEAD DAY | 54
NOW | 55
LIFEWISH | 56
WHO AM I TO DIFFER? | 57
PRISON | 58
TREE | 59
CATCH MAY | 60
BLACK HOURS | 61
SATURDAY NIGHT | 62
SIN | 63

I AM A THOUGHT. | 64
UPHILL, DOWNHILL. | 65
RUNAWAY | 66
THE END | 67
NIGHTMARE | 68
MIRROR | 69
FLOWER POWER | 70
WISHFUL FEELINGS | 71
MISSING | 72
SLEEP | 73
WOMAN | 74
DESERT | 75
NIGHT FLOWER | 77
CHAOS | 78
INSANE | 79
BLACK COFFEE | 80
CHAINS | 81
CEMETERY | 82
DEAD END | 83
RAIN | 84
GHOST | 85
BE ART | 86
HELL | 87
NEVER | 88
STORM | 89
DEVIL STRUCK | 90
THE TIME IS
    TOMORROW | 91
BIGGER THAN LIFE | 92
FLOWERS DO SPEAK | 93
GRAVE | 94
REVOLUTION | 95
TILL | 96
A LOVE | 98
CHIMERA | 99

HARD TIMES | 100
THINKER | 101
DREAMS | 102
NOW | 103
CRY | 104
A DATE | 105
FOR YOU. | 106
LOVE ATTACK | 107
MIND THE MIND | 108
FANTASY | 109
SILENCE | 110
TOGETHER ALONE | 111
HOW CAN | 112
TODAY | 113
ME AND YOU | 114
I AM | 115
YOU | 117
ME, MYSELF AND I | 118
ADVICE | 119
WHY | 120
HUMAN | 121
ROTTEN ROYALS | 123
MEMORY | 124
BLUE | 125
NEW AGE | 127
A SMALL HAPPINESS | 128
NOT IN LOVE | 129
DREAM | 130
THE PROPHECY | 131
UTOPIA | 132
LIVE | 133
BLACK ROSE | 134
TWICE IN A BLUE
    MOON | 135
MY CHRISTMAS | 136

COLORFUL CHRISTMAS | 137
FREEDOM | 138
MY STYLE | 139
MY FRIEND | 140
FACE | 141
MAKE LOVE | 142
THE DIVORCE | 143
JUST BREATHING | 144
DAY | 145
REBORN | 146
BABEL | 147
SAY YOU DO | 148
WHEN MINDS FLY | 149
AWAY | 150
DESTINY | 151
SORROW | 152
THE ENEMY | 153
OUT OF ORDER | 154
OUT OF FAITH | 155
FALLING | 156
GARDEN | 157
FLOWERS | 158
NATURE | 159
FRAGMENTS OF AFTERLIFE | 160

DOING TIME

I am doing my time in this life.
Don't know my crime,maybe it is just afterlife.
Mother is far,far is my heart.
Must be smart but i don't know where to start.

Memory killed by pain,i live under heavy rain.
No sun,no fun,no one
is here with me.I feel like the sea,
all alone,paying for mistakes unknown.

I am doing my time on earth,
been convicted since birth.
Maybe you and me are just the same
but,darling,i don't feel nothing but shame.

For me life is an endless story,
repeats herself with no glory.
Can't escape the invisible chains,
can't scream the unbearable pains.

Doing my time.
For what crime?
Doing my time.
No soul is mine.

DEATH SENTENCE

I am a son behind the sun.
I am a daughter with no water.
I am a man not even humane.
I am a woman stolen by a man.

Living is like a death sentence.
My lips are sealed, can't utter a sentence.
Don't have no tears, to cry my why.
Why i must live and never die.

This heartless life cuts me as a knife.
No blood inside, only fears that i hide.
No God by our side, only our killed pride.
This world is a prison, with no reason.

FATHER

In a miraculous way I found out today,
that I never pray on Sunday.
Broken mirror is my soul, her words left untold,
never been a whole, oh please forgive me Lord.

I see the sky at sea, birds talk about me.
What's her reason, for loosing religion?
Nature is a church, you must ask and search,
for finding His Soul, to the things above.

What's her reason, for loosing religion?

I don't want to ask, never wore a mask.
I don't want to beg, never had a debt.
Doing good is my reaction to evils' action.
I don't say thank you for my life, just in fear for afterlife.

What's her reason, for loosing religion?

I never pray on Sunday.
I find God in every single word
my tears say ·oh LORD, i have lost my way.
Like a refugee, i fled from the land of fidelity.

What's her reason, for loosing religion?

Father, father how can I accept hell,
living without you after your death.
Someone to blame, this is what i am.
After all this pain, life seems so vain.

What's her reason, for loosing religion?

I have lost me, i have lost you, i have lost LORD.
Death has taken my precious soul.
For what to pray, now you are away,
night is the day, now someone must pay.

What's her reason, for loosing religion?
The death of my father, my own conviction.

NOTHING

Nothing happens in my heart.
Monotonous rain fills my path.
Am i a woman, a girl or something?
Setting mind cries i am nothing.

Nothing in my stillness moves.
Feelings, emotions all dead youths.
Am i sea, mountain or moon?
Oh a prisoned dead, happened so soon.

Nothing to think, mind a stranger.
Counting my tears my only pleasure.
Am i the love, the hate, the passion?
Breathing seems to be my only action.

Nothing feels will never cease.
Thoughtless words my chained disease.
Am i me, you or nobody?
Please someone love me to be somebody.

Please someone love me to be somebody. . .

INVISIBLE CAGE

An invisible cage surrounds me.
It is everyday life that devours me.
I live every today like yesterday
and tomorrow will be the same in every way.

An invisible cage is this garden of mine.
Its surroundings the playground of my mind.
Can you hear my crying voice?
Here i am to tell you, life was not my choice.

I was born without knowing.
I am gonna die because of growing.
All of my loved ones will soon be dead
and my tears from God are not heard.

From this circle of everyday, how to be free?
I am a night dressed as day·no longer wanna be.
Just a day in life is my minds' story.
Dead in my heart is my youths' glory.

IN VAIN

My eyes have roots in rain, my plans all in vain.
My bad luck like a chain, leads my heart to pain.
Trying to keep my brain sane,
trying again, lifes' mysteries to explain.

In vain my dark soul cries for freedom.
In vain i wander on this earth like phantom.
In vain i think life is a sanctuary to be adored.
In vain i pray for life eternal for my beloved.

What has Grace against me
and wants to revenge me?
What is my futures' story?
Seems like a deserts territory.

In vain i search for truth by breathing sea.
In vain my eyes turn to sky for God to see.
In vain my heart asks my mind to agree.
In vain. . ..what is to be free? We are all a ground to be.

CONFESSION

From the highlands of my heart to the depths of my soul, i love you.
Trust in me when i say, i will never go away.
From the steps of my past to my hope that we will last, my life depends on you.

Killing me breath by breath, searching your eyes for earth.
I need to be a whole, come on give me your all.
My confession answers your question, will you love me till death? Yes, come on, be my earth.

All of my heart falls apart, when you go away. Please, my thankful soul don't betray.
My tears have the name of you. Oh love, please be true. Like a fairytale me and you, let's our end be ever after a break through.

NIGHT INSIDE

I don't dare to stare at the stars.
My wishes have become my scars.
I don't dare to let my heart pray.
All of my fidelity has fade away.

I tremble in the sight of love.
In any form, love is send from above.
I tremble in the sight of sea.
I am lost in her, myself i can't see.

Does the dog knows a bone is a bone?
Does the tree knows what is a tree?
Does the fish knows it lives in the sea?
Does the bird knows that sky is its home?

In the planet of my mind, God i can find.
In a dog, in a tree, in the sky, at the sea.
In my heart i want to be, where every question has the answer, life is to be free even if you don't know what is to be.

SO ALIKE

Why do flowers wither?
Life for them is like a winter
circling. Never ends.
I have flowers as my friends.

Why the sky is always young?
Birds for its grace sung
this grey and lonely morning.
Sky is my eyes learning.

Why do birds sing?
Is it a message for being
blessed with this earth.
How much we loose from death.

Why does sea cries?
I have a sea inside my eyes
that never sleeps. Only weeps.
Nature and I are so alike.

INSIDE

Oh the sky. . .such a resemblance to my heart. . .
Oh the wind. . .such a match to my mood. . .
Oh the sea. . .such a mate for my mind.
I have nature inside and i didn't even know it. . .

DARLING

Darling, tell the churches to be silent.
Let me hear God speak through birds.
Darling, tell teachers to be on mute.
Let me learn nature by looking at the sea.
Darling, tell politicians to be at last speechless.
Let me live my life with the laws of my heart.
Darling, tell policemen to be humane.
Let me find my way with rights and freedom
Darling, tell mother not to worry.
Let me be myself even if that means living with no glory.
Darling, tell father not to drink.
Let me learn what love is through a family.
Darling, tell God to wake up.
Let me respect Him by respecting animals.
Darling, tell me to shut up.
Let us make our love a new star in the silent sky.

HEART

If my heart had words,
it wouldn't be I love you,
not even how much I miss you.
If my heart had words,
these words would sound like rain,
these words would be my silent pain.

And when the night comes inside,
I have my tears by my side.
That's when my mind starts to mind,
cause I don't know my heart by heart.
That's when my mind loses mind,
cause all I knew as heart was you.
All I knew was you. . .

LONELY

My eyes in another dimension, i only see moving green.
The sky with its red clouds is my private screen.
I barely hear cicadas and my dreams singing.
I am slightly moments away from melting and sinking.
The sweet wind caresses my salty hair
and i just feel love dancing in the colorful air.
My feet walking in the golden sand, while the waves of the sea play like a rock band.
I searched for you. Where have you been?
Ah, you are in the Winter.

EAGLE

An eagle always lives single.
Doesn't fear rain, doesn't care, if life is vain.
An eagle always flies single.
Changes sky,travels till he die.

Above the clouds, avoids the crowds.
Feel his soul,burning like coal.
Abandoned by fiends, his life ends,
with his voice screaming loud, never did he bowed.

An eagle stands always single.
No love can conquer his heart, no one can be more smart.
An eagle always dies single.
His destiny is to be alone, remembering the places he has flown.

BLIND

Is Cupid stupid?
Is Love blind and she can't find,
my soul waiting to be a whole?

Are Muses blind
and they can't see,
the poetry inside of me
that needs to break free?

Is God blind
or he refuses to see,
what humans try to find,
the hunger for Him to be kind?

Are You deaf or blind
and you can't see or hear me?
The feelings that bind me,
myself that kills me?

Just asking. . .

THE AFFAIR

In my crown city, i am the only guilty
for being in love, with a man who is not my own.
Living like a star in day, i want to fly away,
from my hurricane emotions and my soul of oceans.

If love is a game, i will take the blame
cause i played it for life, but you chose your wife.
If memory is prison, i searched for a reason
to let you be with me, if we can't be we.

Am i a bad person or do you give a lesson
on how life is for a good looking miss.
Only my tears love me, when i see what i see,
you with her and me as your affair.

If love is a game, you must take the blame
for losing the key and now i am not free.
I could not forsee, alone that I would be
and you with her together, in love forever.

BEST FRIEND

Capture my words with your mind,
ask and my love you will find.
Search and you will see in the end,
i was always your best friend.

In silence you and me talk loudly.
I see myself in you proudly.
It is like looking in a mirror when i look at you.
It is like having a hero besides me to go this life through.

My best friend from God was send,
to save a life that reached a dead end.
To hear him talk is a lesson to me.
He gives me his eyes when i can't see.

All alone i was without you.
Now you came and shed a light through,
in the darkness of my loneliness.
I am giving you my oniness.

I PRAY

I didn't see the day today.
Closed in my heart, i pray.
For the ones i have lost my pain.
I still love them but in vain.

My eyes turned inside,
don't have anyone by my side.
I turn my hopes to God,
to shed lights on my road.

Fidelity came as a friend,
now my life has reached a dead end.
I pray for my loved ones that are gone.
It is very hard for me to move on.

I pray strongly everyday,
wish my pain would go away.
I pray for loved souls to be forgiven
and to happily live in Heaven.

TV OR NOT TV.

I see my life pass, like an episode of Friends
and my day with TV every night ends.
With the seasons of serials i measure time
and i am telling heroes words, like a mime.

Outside TV life doesn't exist for me.
Countries, people, moon and sea,
i only meet them inside the TV.
I have no complaints, it's a global place to be.

In silence i watch, in silence i live,
in all romance scenarios i do believe.
I fall in love when heroes do.
More alive than me, although nothing true.

No TV is like sentencing me to death,
to all warnings i am completely deaf.
For me the screen is where my life lives,
although my soul truly grieves.

WHITE PAGE

I am searching for little words,
those are said to be swords.
I am searching for broken souls.
Fallen Angel, in hate never falls.

Ordinary things, make me think.
How to put them in the form of my ink?
Ordinary eyes, give me the cries.
The world is a lesson, for an unloved person.

Human poet, search for truth.
Twice in a lifetime, find youth.
The Poet above us Has nature inside.
How to compare with his immaculate light?

Trees are talking, mountains walking.
Sea sleeps, my favorite bird weeps.
My imagination is too small.
To describe this world, is my role.

But the page remains white...
How can i, for my flawless tears, write?
But the page remains white...
Me and words are having a fight.

CYPRESS

Inside this earth i stand i will be
a mortal soul devours me.
The day i die will be no lie
and in this land of trees, i'll have no enemies.

Cypress, Cypress a human less.
You will outlive the human race
with your immaculate grace.
Cypress, Cypress a human less.
No long story and no glory,
to this body which will feed your body.

As proud as you i longed to be.
I thought life's drainless like the sea.
But now i kiss my last breath goodbye
and all my minds ask me why.

Cypress, Cypress a human less
You will live to see the best,
of humankind in future line.
Cypress, Cypress a human less.
Moon, sea, mountains and all the rest
more of me alive, in this ghostly life.

LIFE

Lava coming out of my heart,
volcanic eruption in my mind,
ecstasy while i close my eyes. . .
Just me sitting in the sun.

I see clouds as a fairytale,
what will i read again today?
I hear sea song as my lullaby. . .
Just me before sleeping.

I have Orion as my friend,
stars showing me my way.
I search for moon at day. . .
Just me travelling.

A moment just passed.
Was it my life or will it last?
A moment, i forgot it fast. . .
Just me in life.

MULTIPLE CHOICES

Multiple choices in my mind,
for what to do, for what to leave behind.
Multiple choices in my heart,
all i want is to be a kind of art.

Like in a garden gazing flowers,
i am lost in choices for hours.
Will i be good or bad, smart or fool,
i want emotions to take the rule.

Fearless i must stand in front of myself,
don't want to be left on the shelf.
I have choices to be with you or not,
i have the choice to solve my lifes' knot.

Multiple tears cry for my future,
lost as in an uncharted picture.
I am lost in my mind but i still have choices,
to leave myself completely voiceless.

A WALK

Wild flowers in the field, nothing that they need.
How i wish i was like them, how i wish i was a natures gem.
Being free and peaceful, with life so full.
Being in my role,to bring beauty to the world.

Wild flowers in the field, now in my hands they are held.
A sweet memory of nature, a colorful momenture.
Powerful they are although so weak,
do flowers cry or do they speak?
Joy they give, what joy they get, what is their souls secret debt?

Wild flowers in the field, i am from my heart so healed.
Only the silence of the wind is heard and the love wounded bird.
I want my hand to touch the sky, why we must die?
Like a flower i once was young and by nature i was drunk.

INVISIBLE

I feel invisible in here, nobody to hear,
my crying voice, my dead end choice,
to write my feelings, which need healings.
Maybe writing in verse is my curse.

Invisible is my middle name, don't know the game,
but it hurts so much to be out of touch.
Nobody to see your heart, nobody to read your mind.
Life is cruel, lonely and blind.

Doesn't see the pain in me,
doesn't give me a reason to be.
Like the wind i wish to blow away my invisibility,
to find again my living ability.

Invisible is like having a thorn in the head,
which causes a lot of hurt.
What's the use of being true and kind,
when the other says "never mind"?

FREE BIRDS

Hungry birds wait for Spring.
Love songs always sing.
Fly from tree to tree,
oh, life can be so free.

No mother, no father,
no sister and brother.
Only anonymous friends
and singing life till it ends.

Perpetual moving,
hard is the living.
Starving for food
but free is still good.

No love connection,
no cage detention.
Freedom in natures' kingdom,
beauty they bring as they sing.

Life is free but dangerous,
maybe the cage would be more safe.
Life free is treacherous,
needs one to be smart and brave.

Free birds are just a moment
in our life. But bring such delight.
Does their life end,
with tears that never came in sight?

Do birds cry?

THE LIFE I HAD

You may say I look like mad
or even think I am truly bad.
But I am just a simple sad
cause I miss the life I had.

When I was twenty, my hair were long, black and plenty
and at my thirty, my middle name was mister flirty.

Around my forty, my pretty wife became my life
and at my fifty, I was the dad and Santa Gifty.

Oh sometimes, how I miss the life I had, when I used to have a dad.
Oh sometimes, how I miss my lonely me, the one I had before the we.

Oh sometimes, how I miss our first kiss, when loving you was a wish.
And sometimes, I truly wonder if you miss, the time you were a dreamy miss.

You may say I am mister no,
cause I say I don't know,
when you ask me why I am sad,
maybe I miss the life I had.

THE CAT

I am a stray cat, looking for a rat.
All day i am wandering around, making peculiar sound.
In my head love is dead.
Can decide, live or die?

Searching for food is my everyday route
and my other thoughts are on mute.
Life for me is a losing game, full of pain.
Can decide, cry or fly?

Playing with the sun, trying to have fun.
Forgetting i am hungry and with God so angry.
Where is my mother, why i don't have a father?
Can decide, scream or dream?

Facing secret dangers, touched by strangers.
Why was i born, why i was in this world thrown?
My eyes meet the sky, how i wish i could fly.
Can decide, live or die?

CAGE

I read between your eyes
the unbearable lies.
My pure heart deeply cries.
Wish she could be more wise.

Freedom is my new cage.
Being alone makes me outrage.
I am afraid of my age.
Must turn my lifes' page.

Cage is my dark mind.
Always in front of life blind.
I need a new love to find,
i need someone who will be kind.

How can i escape the cage of myself?
My road leads me to a lonely shelf.
How can i escape the cage of life,
who orders a woman to become a wife?

SUCCESS STORY

As she returns home, nobody there,
she feels that her loneliness is unfair.
As she goes to bed not even dreams approach her.
Life a heavy burden she no longer knows how to bear.

She must smile to prove she is happy,
when all she needs it is her daddy.
She must go out and fancy mingle,
when she must hide she is still single.

Money buys her clothes and things
but where she can sell her soul she thinks,
to find a happy family and true love.
She constantly prays to her Angels above.

Glamorous and luxurious her life,
but all she wants is to be a wife.
Unloved and betrayed is her story,
full of success but without true glory.

AT LAST

The silence of the butterflies
is the beauty of my todays' eyes.
Fallen angels in disguise,
in their wings i see again that God is wise.

At last, silence speaks its secrets.

The silence of the dancing trees
my minds at war please, with peace.
Nature is my only true friend.
Never will die, never will meet the end.

At last, a friend that speaks the truth.

The silent question to be asked
is where is my soul inside me?
All my thoughts travel so fast.
Trying to find where God sleeps without me.

At last, a moment that will last.
My death.

THE YEAR

I won't change the year this year,
i will stop counting the time of my life from fear,
of getting old, of dying all alone.
I am wondering where have my dreams gone?

I won't change the year this year,
now even my tear is truly clear.
I cry for the heart i have lost,
i cry for the ones that grieved me most.

I won't change the year this year,
i will be having my thoughts near.
Me and my mind will be just fine,
living from the whole world one year behind.

CREMATION

I don't want to be buried, i want to be free.
Let me burn and spread my ashes to the sea.
If we all live in Gods' dream, let me wake Him up,
let Him see how life after death has turned up.

I bury seeds to give me trees, i bury
flowers to give me beauty, i bury
dreams deep down my heart, i bury
my every day to the yesterday that's gone with no sorry.

But i don't want to be buried, my body is no flower
to grow. Oh how i wish i had the power,
never to have been born, if only i knew,
what life means to go through.

My cremation will be my last wish
and the unexistence will be my bliss.
Life is a very heavy burden for me,
let me and my ashes be part of the sea.

NET

Our planet is the internet,
and I am an alien in net.
Fax me, email me, friend me and like me,
join me and follow, read me and write me.
See me and hear me, vote me and note me,
search me and learn me, rate me and suggest me.

Our planet is the internet,
and I am an alien in net.

I am out of age, for my age,
and my time has no time.
Past is past all so fast
nothing will last, that's a must.

I live the days of the TV or not TV
and that we agree we disagree.
Caught in the net of internet
where my life is out of life.

Our planet is the internet
and I am an alien in net,
just an alien in internet.

Be in the book, to have a look,
send me a tweet, oh you are so sweet.
Have my profile in your favorite file,
let's meet in your page, oh what a lonely age.

Our planet is the internet
and I am an alien in net,
just an alien in internet.

IRONY

It is a pity that i am pretty
but no one looks at me.
It is a pity that i am sweety
but no one kisses me.

I am so lonesome and i want some,
love and affection.
I am so awesome and i want some,
passion and attention.

I am in fashion, wear some passion,
to be pretty in the city.
I am so noble, all so global
and in my heart, i am art.

There are voices, just pure noises,
that talk back to me.
But i am perfect, in every aspect,
would you fall in love with me?

MY CASE

I rest my case, she is now sleeping,
moments ago she was weeping.
My voice has said my hearts' mind,
i don't care, if you don't mind.

My case is being me with no fear,
i don't want my eyes to lose another tear.
My case is being free of darkness,
this life to leave me completely harmless.

Seas away from God, i am afraid
my soul has overpaid
this life of misery and pain.
All is vain, what is it to gain?

People inside me try to be me,
my case is to find a simple way to be.
I rest my soul, she now sleeps.
For how much eternity life keeps?

THE CHANGE

To change the hardest thing
to change I fear to think.

Will be my heart and mind
or will I be smart and kind,
must change my ways and says,
or must I be we instead of me.

To change the hardest thing,
to change where to begin.
To change the hardest thing,
to change I fear to think.

A yes sir they want me to be,
a yes sir to let me free.
A yes sir for the society,
a yes sir with no honesty.

Will be my life and style
or just my wife and time.
Will change my home and work
what must I do to learn the homework.

DIE

I look at the sunny sky,
i wish i will never die.
This idea penetrates my soul,
how can i leave this world?

Don't want to be fertile ground,
don't want my soul to leave with a wound.
Don't want to meet God,
i will have to confess a lot.

My eyes cry as i pray,
don't want to die, i must find a way.
The loved ones i will leave behind,
a thorn always in my mind.

I am a sinner but i am not afraid,
for my soul i have already prayed.
I am afraid of the cold darkness,
i don't want to live as heartless.

SOLITUDE

In solitude i found my attitude.
Loneliness became a kind of mood.
It is not a brief interlude
but a state where my mind is glued.

I fear to let my heart feel.
She is my Achilles' heel.
From life has kneeled
and she never healed.

I fear to have a connection.
My mind has lost his affection.
I am looking for perfection,
searching for Gods' reflection.

In solitude i have my tears.
Their silent shout nobody hears.
They cry for my fears
that all alone i will be throughout the years.

WE ARE

We are just the opposite,
that's why we'll never meet.
I like the rain, you like to gain,
I like the sun, you like to tun.

You like the meat, I like the wheat,
you like the wine, I like the vine.
We are just the opposite,
so when are we gonna meet…cause…

We are the ones, who'll fight to be one,
we are the hearts, who can beat like one.
We are the ones, around us there's none,
we are the halfs that can make the one.
We are just the opposite,
that's why we'll never meet.

You like the ride, I like to ride,
you like to see, I like to be.
I like to run, you like to can,
I like to know, you like the no.

HEAVY RAIN

Wasting time is my middle name,
seems life is a boring game.
Needs two to be cleverly played
but i am all alone and my years fade.

Darkness in my heart although it's day,
maybe i must learn how to pray.
For nothing around me interests me,
nothing around me cares for me.

I feel under heavy, heavy rain,
no rainbow will be my gain.
Like a barren earth, i have
only my tears that misbehave.

Heavy rain, rain again against me,
you and me lost in the lifes' sea.
We are only made from tears,
you and me together for so many years.

POETRY

Poetry is a tree.
Do believe in me.
Has her roots at sky
and wings to fly.

Words her teardrops.
Rhyme her crime.
Feelings her healings.
Thoughts her knots.

Poetry is a tree.
Every morning kissing me.
Let our Love be.
Let her set me free.

She is a tree at sea.
Sailors all we.
Ship the world we live.
In poetry i do believe.

Like a statue of nature,
has a mind so mature,
a heart so delicate,
oh yes, in silence we communicate.

Poetry is a tree.
Give her dreams to be
and you will suddenly see,
mountains having sea.

I am in love with poetry.
We have a lighting chemistry.
Star is her middle name
oh me, a lover of her game.

TEARS

Isolation inside my mind,
i am running from life behind.
Never more in need for a friend,
never more closer to the end.

My eyes only for tears are here,
their silent voice nobody to hear.
My heart has lost her place
and i am just an alien in space.

I feel my feelings exhausted
and my body is still haunted,
by isolation and rejection.
I am in desperate need of affection.

No use to count my thoughts,
my mind tied in knots.
No use to feel my breath,
only tears i will leave on this earth.

SAVE THE DATE

Save the date, don't be late,
to a life that is going to be great.
Hold your heart, move your head,
just be smart and get off bed.

Save the date, don't be late,
to find the gate where lucks await.
Burry hate, find a soul mate,
lose hearts' freight, heaven is straight.

Save the date, don't be late,
to have a blind date with fate.
Be strongly brave, don't wait,
find the way to be great.

Save the date, don't be late,
angels wait for you to wake.
Save the date for something great,
be the hero of your fate.

HOUSEWIFE

I always took sea for granted
just like my life.
But an accident happened
and i became a housewife.

I thought dreams are like sky,
which gives birth to clouds.
But now i am around plates,
counting my hidden wounds.

I am no Shakespeare,
i know it for sure.
But i always thought i could
write something good,
to escape me from my
to be or not to be situation.
Now in the sink
suicides my salvation.

Life slipped from my mind
and now she is not mine.
How can i free myself
or invent a new one instead?

Cause i am fed up
with housekeeping, ironing,
washing and cooking.
Cause i am fed up
with listening in silence
and trying to keep the balance.

Cause i am fed up
with me and i want to be free,
to change my world.
Oh Lord, make me say the word.
Let me. . .

NEW YEAR, MY DEAR

Will I have a sweetheart in my heart
or will I be alone drinking in the dark.
Will I see my eyes in anothers' eyes
or will my mirror say, just another bad day.

But, don't you worry, I'll be the sorry,
for my new year's story, has no Santa glory.

New year, my dear,
there is nothing new in my tear.
New year, my dear,
your days and nights my new fear.

So. . .new year, my dear,
have a happy new year.

Will I start to have my new ends
or will my habbits stay my old friends.
Will I feel my heart in anothers' hug
or will I be again with my old bad luck.

FOOL STOP

My mind tries to put a full stop,
to thoughts that make me a fool.
I need my heart to be on top,
so i can bare life that's cruel.

Fool, stop, cries my mind,
but i don't hear, i leave him behind.
Full stop i will put to my expectations
i don't need a life of complications.

Laughing although crying, crying although laughing.
This is the state of everyday person
in everyday life, always fearing and hiding.
Doesn't want to be another lesson.

Having the heart in the right side
always ready for an unknown fight.
Having the mind always on mute
searching for the forgotten root.

Fool, stop, put a full stop to hypocrisy.
Dare to have a soul democracy,
so heart and mind won't be enemies
but good, loving equities.

SUN AND RAIN

Sun and rain, come out again,
give me something for the pain.
Make me forget that life is hurt,
make me forget my broken heart.

As opposites attract somehow,
i need to find my other half now.
To be in life alone and crying,
what is the difference from dying?

Sun and rain, you are humane.
You came and ease my pain.
Tears and smile, they are so alike.
When one comes, the others hide.

Life be sweet, i am just a heartbeat,
don't want this pain, to go in vain.
Life be kind, i am one of a kind
and i always have love in my mind.

DEAD DAY

I see my pen and i want to write
but i see my mind and i want to cry.
Unfortunately i don't have a high mind,
of intellectual quality i am still behind.

Words are my prison, i have lost the key.
To find a new reason, my way to be.
I am full of sorrow, wish i had apathy.
I need a mind to borrow, in lack of fantasy.

Oh Muses, bring me inspiration,
give me ways to find a new destination.
I see my pen and i want to cry.
So many questions, no answer to why.

Dead are my days when i can't write.
No use to have my usual soul fight.
I am the one to blame, i know it for sure.
I have nothing to write and there is no cure.

NOW

Now you see me, now you don't.
I don't care if you say i am not,
the cool girl you will love to love a lot.
All i know is that in my net you are caught.

Now you feel me, now you don't.
You are just my minds' knot.
Although you say i am what you sought,
your eyes lie and that's not my thought.

Now you need me, now you don't.
You must know you are not my want.
I always for liberty fought
and you are just another fault.

Now you hear me, now you don't.
You did all and everything wrong.
Now you want me, now you don't.
I don't care, alone i am not. . .

I've got myself to live for,
i've got myself to fight for,
i've got myself to smile for.
I've got myself to love.

LIFEWISH

For your kiss, i have a lifewish.
Be my heartbeat, make me complete.
For your eyes, my melancholy dies.
Walk me to a star, how similar we are.

I am breathing the sky, my wings fly.
I am touching the sun, to be me i can.
I am winning the world, my heart i hold.
I don't have the need, in everything to succeed.

To find my bliss,i have a lifewish.
I will not miss, my minds abyss.
To find my way, i am flying away.
In a new love, i got what i want.

I have a lifewish for kissing life.
Everything is in the mind
and the secret is to find,
the way to leave death behind.

WHO AM I TO DIFFER?

Sea is where you swim but you can drown also.
Rain is a melancholy pleasure but it can be a menace also.
Fire warms you but you can burn also.
Forest is where you go for a walk but you can be lost also.
Wind can come as a sweet breeze but it can cause destructions also.
Lightning is a charming sight to see but it can kill you also.
Night is a romantic place to be but you can't be safe also.
Sun can warm you but it can burn you also.

Everything in nature has its good and bad self.

Who am i to differ?

PRISON

To be in prison, is a human condition.
But isn't also a tree, bind to itself and not free?
To be in prison, is living with no reason.
But isn't also thoughts, the cages built by our words?

I always felt that life is a prison, that ends with death.
Counting the moments, nights and days with every breath.
Can't escape life otherwise, the solution is to be wise.
Having yourself as a friend, living with dreams that have no end.

I am caged to myself, can't be another woman.
I am born a human, can't be an animal or plant.
I am destined to have as a wife or as a partner a man.
I am born this way, to differ i can't.

Is my nature my prison?
Is this world my prison?
Is it myself i can't escape
or is it life that i am afraid?

TREE

My tree is the key to be free.
I forget to be me.
In solitude i watch the birds
singing for its grace
as they linger in its embrace.
I listen to their song and it helps.
To ease the pain i feel inside.
I wonder, where my tree
hides its mind?
It is a romantic sight to see,
under its shadow to be.
Like a green sea it dances
with the wind and suddenly everything is kind.
A new me every time i see
my singing tree.

CATCH MAY

I want to catch May, if i may.
Flowers around me always young.
I want to live with them this day.
It is no secret, Summer has sprung.

From darkness i rise with hope.
Maybe this May will be my home.
For a new beginning i am looking
and the past behind me i am locking.

Winter inside me has its roots
but today i am gonna fly away.
No longer need for boots,
i am wearing summer in my heart and i am ok.

May, oh May be my friend.
Put in my melancholy an end.
Bring the sun and sea to me.
Let me live at last from phantoms free.

BLACK HOURS

Black hours count my time,
hating cruel life my crime.
My heart is a small runaway
from this dead end day.

Black hours face my fate,
feeling nothing but hate.
For my destiny is death.
Can't change my end.

Black hours stand like a human.
Watching my life without a man.
Solitude and silence are my friends,
in a circle of lives that never ends.

Black hours make me cry.
There is a world inside me that screams why.
Why am i weak and afraid to live.
Why can't i my poor self forgive.

SATURDAY NIGHT

A rainbow stares at me, born from my coffee glass.
I smoke my cigarette with a black and white attitude.
I dress myself like painting a melancholic canvas.
I am under self and world destructive mood.

The night hides my injured feelings
and the tears that run like warm sea from my eyes.
I am counting wounds that need healings,
as i walk out the door, another guilty day dies.

Saturday night like a big, awkward theater stage,
with actors forgetting their small role.
Another night, another empty page,
another dive to my hearts black hole.

As i return to my home, i feel alone.
Myself on mute, my favorite suit.
My dreams left me, they are now gone.
And me, here in the death of the night,
eating passion fruit.

SIN

I am writing for all the dead ants, their death being a tear in my eyes.

It is a sin, to walk on small animals indifferent for their pain.
But who is the sinner here?

Ants, cockroaches, spiders, flies.
Each of them from human dies.
Who is there to cry for them?
Who is their suffocating why to hear?

What is their purpose on life?
To put more sins on humans soul?
To live their life without a voice and choice?

God is absent from their life and death.
Thus humans become murderers at an instant.

I am just walking but in the same time i am killing ants which i can't see.

Is that a sin?
Or is it God's sin?

Am i too blind to see the reason
behind the unreasonable?

Just thinking. . ..

I AM A THOUGHT.

Tonight i was a thought in somebodys' mind.I didn't sleep.
The persistent song of the birds brought me back to my reality.
Here all of my feelings are deep
and my mind lost in serenity.

I am a thought built from silent words.
A thought as one of the trillions Gods' works.
I enter dreams that tears wake up.
I create worlds that never start.

I am a constant thought in my mothers' mind.
And you can also search in silence to find,
the true beginning of my body.
I can capture and live in everybody.

I come in peace but war is my religion.
Life collapsing under my pressure is my vision.
Erupting souls and reborn minds
is my purpose and what, with me, one finds.

I am a thought. Aren't we all?

UPHILL, DOWNHILL.

My life is an uphill. Has been also a downhill.
But now, i can't keep the balance any more.
Don't know how, don't have the strength, the will.
Wish i knew for what way to fight for.

There is the way of virtue and vice.
Which to pick you must think twice.
The one, the hard one, leads to your soul.
The other, the easy one, makes your soul a fool.

Each path you will take, somewhere will take you.
The journey will teach you to be yourself,
cause in the end accountable will be you and only you.
When one is lost inside him, how can he find himself?

Uphill and downhill are the two faces of living.
All has to do with the mind and soul giving.
Virtue can give you heart bleeding awareness.
Vice can give you the absolute nothingness.

The choice is yours.

RUNAWAY

I am a runaway from this lonesome June.
I want to run to September, where my feelings remember
you. You my graceful, starless moon.
Now i am so closed to me, with you i was so tender. Remember?

My heart flies away from my body,
to my past, when i used to be somebody.
There my life had a purpose, you.
Today i have no one, so sad but true.

I have a runaway mind, that leaves me behind.
Leaves me alone with the winds of despair.
I do search but never find,
a new start, some fresh air.

I have a runaway mood towards my destiny.
Don't want to meet it, don't want to know it.
All i want is to be loved, to get through this eternity.
All i want is from myself to quit.

THE END

Are we like God? Then, what is cruelty doing among us?
I see her everywhere i look. In nature, in working places, between us.
Are we like Angels? Then, why do we kill each other?
We are in desperate need of love and of a father.

If the end was near, we all would be on our knees, uttering prayers.
Others would be drinking, counting their blessings and their money. Oh such liars.
Some just to be sure, there would be making love for the last time.
As for me, the coming of the end, wouldn't mean a dime.

Cause with every breath, i wish for an end.
In a life that can't be mend and is misspend,
the end seems so inviting. Even challenging.
I would escape from this living.

But the end, my friend, will never come.
And cruelty, killings, life will overcome
any judgement day. Life will keep its way.
The end as we know it is death. Is death the end?

NIGHTMARE

How far is my dream from nightmare?

I dreamed of being a black sea. Oh freedom, one could think. Oh solitude, the other.

I dreamed of being a winter's sky. Oh, so close to God. So far from humans.

I was an apple tree. So splendid with its fruits. So alone.

I dreamed of being dead. Now i will meet God. Now God will meet me.

How far is my dream from nightmare?

MIRROR

Mirror, mirror on the wall,
who is the cruelest of them all?
Is it God, Satan or Human?
God made nature, Satan made it jungle and human the killer.
Where is God?
God made sea, Satan made waves and human the killer.
Where is God?
God made animals, Satan gave the instinct and human the killer.
Where is God?
God made human, Satan made love and human the killer.
Where is God?

FLOWER POWER

It is not hard to see that we are guests here.
In my heart i know i am here to show
to the world that a word has power.
Even the one coming from a flower.

Flower power is the essence of giving
without asking back. The true meaning of forgiving.
To be beautiful without knowing it,
to be useful without bragging about it.

Words coming from flowers are silent.
It is their smell, their tender body.
Flowers are never violent
and they love everybody.

Flower power will outlive all of us.
Good and beauty in this world will last.
As long as we take lessons from nature
and we live life like childs' mature.

WISHFUL FEELINGS

Oh how i wish i was young again,
with todays' brain.
I wouldn't go in vain,
wouldn't have spent my time in pain.

I miss the time of my youth,
when every lie brought a new truth.
I miss the time i was a child,
when i was like nature, free and wild.

I am old enough now to know,
that when you are young you wish to grow.
But when you are old and your death is near,
oh poor feelings, you are nothing but fear.

Wishful feelings come on embrace me.
Let us be brave in front of the grave.
Come on give me a reason free to be
from my past, where i still play, laugh and run fast.

MISSING

My heart is missing from my body.
I have lost my best buddy.
To her i turned when night came,
to her i cried when loosing lifes' game.

How can i go on as a heartless being,
what will be my meaning?
From my feelings labyrinth how can i be free,
now that i don't have a heart to guide me?

In her i could find my instinct, my soul.
Now in the place of her there is a hole.
I am searching in life to find a substitute.
Must change my attitude.

Here i am crying for the death of her.
Feeling like a living monster.
Here i am dead and not lying
and i can hear my heart laughing.

SLEEP

Sleep is the twin brother of death.
Every night i follow the dream path.
Am i a dream in Gods' mind
or am i dreaming that this life is mine?

Necrophania is what i am afraid the most.
To wake up in the grave...there i would be lost.
What can one do when although dead still alive?
What can one do when his dreams are from life more alive?

Sleep is where i escape from myself.
There i say to life farewell.
Multiple personalities i have, multiple lives i live,
all in one moment. Oh, for being in a constant good dream what could i give.

I would give up TV, music and books.
I would give up Nature and my looks.
Cause in a dream i feel more alive from alive.
There living has a meaning. I search for the meaning of life.

WOMAN

I am a woman murdered by a man.
Hear my voice to know, i didn't have a choice.
I was born in this life to unwillingly be a wife.
I was made a mother, before knowing my father.
I lived under cruelty and pain and all my tears went in vain.
I am a woman but above all i am human.
I rest in no peace, as my torture will not cease,
until men understand that we won't accept being treated inhumane.
World must know, that no is a no.
My heart goes for all of you, who have walked in my shoe.
Life for a wife must be love and not a boxing glove.
Hear my voice, you now have a choice.
Leave, if you want to live.

DESERT

A desert is my soul.
A quicksand my dreams.
A nothing is my expectations.
A thick silver my silence.

I feel evil around me.

A desert my life.
Searching for an oasis
in your eyes.
All of my feelings is hurt
and pain is my only gain.

I feel evil around me.

A desert in the city is my life,
living just to be a wife.
I am a woman and a human,
i have wrongs and rights.

I feel evil around me.

I am a black desert in need of a rain.
No, i will not go in vain.
I will have a flower and a tree,
i will be from my destiny free.

NIGHT FLOWER

I am a night flower, sleeping all day
but when the sun sets and everyone is at their beds,
i shine like a star and leave at night my scar.
All atmosphere from me smells like heaven and with me there is no even.

I am a night flower dressed in black,
i have feelings lost and dark.
My body, so beautiful, strangers attracks
but for me love is nothing but an attack.

I am a night all day long
and to myself i belong.
Have no masters, love only God
and to hide my soul i am taught.

I am a flower anyone can pick
but before touching me one should think.
Can i have her now and later on
or shall i leave her to her beauty all alone?

CHAOS

Chaos is myself, intense darkness inside me.
Wish i was free from me, i wish somebody else to be.
I don't know me anymore, i can't find the door
that leads to my heart, to my soul.

Chaos is the past years inside me.
Can't seem to find reason, can't be free
from the skeletons of the past.Oh, myself will last
till eternity i feel. How i wish i could turn the wheel
of time and change heart, change mind.

Chaos is my feelings for my loved ones.
Love and hate change at once
and i don't know what to do with me.
My mood changes like a wavy sea.

Chaos is the world i live.
Wish i could just walk and leave
from my life but i can't. I have roots in her. Can't seem with her to have a truce.

INSANE

Insane, shout the voices in my head.
Thoughts, memories, fantasy and feelings so complicated.
And from outer life so intoxicated.
Somedays i don't even get out of bed.
But you know, truly, i have got something new to say.
Be a child all the way.
And if this means walking barefoot on cold sand or having a leaf shower or dancing, like there is no tomorrow, under heavy snow, then do it.
Insane, you are an insult to your family. A fault, a disgrace for humanity. But i don't care. I laugh loudly as i burst in tears. You know Insane is the name of my heart.

What can i do?
Does your heart have a name?

BLACK COFFEE

Black coffee is my food,
i have from time lost my mood.
Nothing for me seems to be quite good,
in this death way that is my route.
I don't know, maybe remembering myself i should.

From the times i was young and beautiful
and from love so full.
From the times that tomorrow meant another world,
not like now, that i can't utter a new word.

Black coffee is my close hearted friend,
now that everything around me shouts for an end.
Gives me a reason to wake up, a reason to stay awake. It is black coffee i am never gonna give up.

CHAINS

I am like a prisoner in chains.
This life gives me all kind of pains.
Pain for the death of my father,
was my whole life, i have no other.

Pain for everyday that life dies.
Memories only left from time that flies.
Pain for every breath that leads me to death.
Oh this life, brings out the most of my wrath.

Chains are my feelings and thoughts.
Tide me down like locked knots.
They make it impossible to change.
Like in a prison i am fighting with chains.

My soul like Prometheus fights to break free.
It is not wind. It is made of sea.
Carries me away but all suddenly stops.
My chains hold me to the ground, like roots.

CEMETERY

My thoughts dead, buried in the cemetery of my mind.
Walking around them, reminds me of years behind.
My feelings suicide from the hills of my heart.
Buried inside me, i look at them, like looking at art.

Lost inside me, i understand there is only pain.
From past and present years, i have only tears.
Dead inside me are my wishes and my love plan.
Oh life, you are nothing but everyday death to the mortal man.

In a cemetery, where like statues, lay human,
i come in peace with the fact that life is inhumane.
We are all destined to have our last home there.
What good can i do to souls with a prayer?

Cemetery, cemetery you are for every
one of us a home. Even for the homeless.
But i carry one inside and now i am heartless.
Death and i such friends. Oh cemetery, my cemetery.

DEAD END

It is six o'clock and i am still a rock,
petrified by fear and isolation.
My father dead and i am lost in dread,
swimming in the sea of desperation.

It is like i am in a new life after his death
and all the tears come with every breath.
I feel like a baby alone and afraid,
how will his love be replaced?

Like in a dead end way i am walking.
Trees mourn and birds are talking.
In my fantasy, where memories stay, i live
and i see that my days and nights silently leave.

Dead end my friend is the circle of life,
no use to argue with God and strife.
We will all end in the dark afterlife
and if we are good maybe turn up as trees in the wildlife.

RAIN

Rain coming from my eyes, two green skies,
waiting for a rainbow to shine and glow.
All of my feelings are rain, gone in vain.
Wasted love for the one i used to adore.

Rain talking with me, as i am all alone.
Thoughts and right words all gone.
Myself an empty cell, mind escaped
to a place where rain is from heart seperate.

Rain falling inside me, like a warm silent, black sea.
Everywhere i turn my eyes, only you i see
and tears make me blind.
What to search for? Where can one mind find?

Rain has become my best friend.
Silent, listening to me, holding my hand.
In my heart i want to hide
but i have lost her too. Lost my pride.

GHOST

I am a withered tree, a drained sea.
I am a ghost forgotten in an isolated coast.
My lips never smile, my eyes never cry.
With every breath, i wish for death.

I am a depressed shadow and all i know,
is that i am nothing but a now.
Have no future and no past
and this through eternities will last.

Once upon a time i had a life.
Used to be a human and i was a wife.
But dead now i am from my man's hand.
He left me and killed my heart.

If only i knew that love will be the death of me,
all alone and loveless i would be.
Now i am a now without freedom,
searching for myself in this broken kingdom.

BE ART

It is your destiny to fly. Don't walk.
It is your dream to write. Don't talk.
It is your passion to be art. Work with your heart.
It is your plan to be somebody. Be your buddy.

Do something that will make you think
out of the ordinary. Be for life hungry.
Do what your instinct tells you to do.
Don't be blue. Just every moment brand new.

It is your destiny to sing. Don't speak.
It is your dream to work. Be an artwork.
It is your passion to be free. Be a sea.
It is your plan to love you more. Don't be a bore.

Do to yourself what from others you desire.
Burn your past in your soul fire
and try to go from life much higher.
Dare yourself to love, honor and admire.

HELL

In mighty Hell is where i dwell and all is well.
Living underneath the world without uttering a word.
But you know, being dead doesn't mean you don't have a life.
It is simply called the afterlife.

I am a dead man walking, working without smoking.
I can't see how i look, i do everything by the book.
I am paying for my sins and yes the Angel always wins.
The worst is the eternities of time that go by, waiting to pay my crime.

And after Hell what? Another Life?
No thank you. Been there, done that.
Been to both worlds and for what?
To end as an animal in the wildlife.

When time ends, when sea dies?
When sky collapses, when God cries?
I am wondering, is there an end to existence in any form
or we are doomed endlessly to transform?

NEVER

As right as rain were my feelings for you.
Hidden in a small cloud inside me, waiting for you to come true.
But you never came, i was left with shame.
My soulful wishes all went in vain.

Better never than late, i am thinking,
while my tears do the speaking.
If i knew that love was never meant to be,
i wouldn't spent my time waiting for her. Like waiting for the death of sea.

Never again will i fall in love. Maybe i will fall in hate.
With life, that never gave me a dreamy date.
With me, that never found the power to be me.
With you, that never gave me love but left me deep blue.

Never seems so little, in comparison with my rage.
Maybe not accepting life any more is an attitude of age.
But all i know is that never will i love,
till the sweet time i will go above.

STORM

I am caught in the middle of a heart storm.
Feelings fighting to break free from me.
It is like i am lost in an inside sea,
where everything is cold, ugly and wrong.

I am having again my usual brain storm.
Thoughts, plans, memories and words, fight with swords.
My brain like a rainy,cloudy, dark sky,
says its goodbye,
while i am losing faith and i am standing all alone.

My soul gives her fight like caught in a tormentous storm.
Wants to escape from her prison, my body.
If i loose her, i will feel like a nobody.
Having her always made me feel strong.

I am living a life full of silent storms.
Death and loss, pain me the most.
If as they say, we learn from tragedy,
i have learned to escape from life, with fantasy.

DEVIL STRUCK

I am a devil struck. You can imagine my luck.
In a world build for immaculate angels,
i am turning my back and i wear only black.
Me and God are completely strangers.

Being a devil is always bad. Makes me sad.
Been this way since birth and after dying i will continue to be one.
Not that my cruelty makes me glad
but when you are born a devil how can his fate change one?

My usual way is cursing all day.
I am not much of a worker, mostly a joker.
My heart is absent, my soul gone
and as for my mind cuts a bone.

Me, myself and I, a mysterious team.
Some say "oh, a devil" and they are afraid.
Some, at the sight of me, do scream.
But this is their fate. With me they get paid.

THE TIME IS TOMORROW

Today the time is tomorrow, for life to be lived.
I have shut my heart. She has for long been deceived.
Canceling myself and my life is my usual way.
Tomorrow maybe i will fly away.

The time is never now, to be loved more.
We forget to live, cause we have tomorrow.
Life some days is such a bore.
But we neglect that all is left is sorrow.

Today is not the time for being you.
It is not even the time for the things you want to do.
We all know that this is not true.
Cause tomorrow might never come on view.

Now is so precious, there will be no other.
It is like sisters, brothers and mother. We have no other.
Love and live like there is no tomorrow,
is the solution for living a life that someone would like to borrow.

BIGGER THAN LIFE

What is bigger than life? Death.
Holds until the Second Advent.
If there is Paradise and Hell,
there souls live into their cell.

What is bigger than life? My mother.
Gave me birth and will be inside me until my death.
Like her there is, for each one of us, no other.
I owe her every single breath.

What is bigger than life? Nature.
Mountains, sea and moon, will be here through eternity.
Like an undying, mature and lonely creature,
she will be here to see our final entity.

What is bigger than life? Written Words.
Thoughts formed into written galaxies,
will be standing like mighty Lords.
The future will outlive all fantasies.

FLOWERS DO SPEAK

I heard them today, kissing the sun good morning.
They are so sweet as their cute yawing.
They whisper, because they don't want nobody to hear,
but it is so simple. All it takes is to be near.

To listen with the depths of your heart.
Their song, so melodic, just pure art.
So velvet, their beautiful petal.
So funny, they like heavy metal.

Flowers do speak, although so weak.
Their perfumed voice says, we are a beauty choice.
To make your day, like a fairytale all the way.
You know, flowers have secret powers.

For hours i can listen to their song.
They keep me company all day long.
Their beauty is my wish for me.
As sweet and lovely as them i want to be.

GRAVE

Once in the grave, one must be brave.
The Creator he will meet, he will be at his feet.
Once in the grave, he'll be asked how he behaved
and all he will utter is, God save me, save.

The moment of my death speaks a lot to me.
It will be the time i will be from life free.
For me dying is the end of lying.
It is the time i will have my greatest greeting.

I am not afraid of the grave, of death
which i think with every breath.
I am not afraid of meeting God.
It will be like meeting a Father, not that i am bold.

But the sorrow i will cause to the ones that love me,
frightens me. What is lifes' meaning
when all ends at a hole, surpasses me.
Maybe all has to do with love giving.

Maybe. . . .

REVOLUTION

Revolution is the solution,
to save our planet home.
To escape from the pollution,
no need from mask to mask to roam.

Revolution of the mind,
to leave politicians behind
and be political correct. For the planet
we must build a security net.

Understand that our breaths depend from our actions.
Our life can cause ecosystem destructions.
Our heart must empathize with this story.
Our future, if we don't act, will have no glory.

A planet is in need, no voice to speak.
But those who hear its silent tears,
care for the environment that's weak.
Love mother Earth and eco revolt now, so never to live our worst fears.

Plant a tree, to be free.
Be ethical, use no chemical.
Use the bicycle and recycle.
Be loving and good
to animals. They are not your food.

TILL

My mind walks
among the valley of thoughts.
Picks some like flowers
and holds them for hours.

But...

Till the sun dies
and the sea dries,
my mind will think of you.
Till the moon dives
and the night lights,
my heart will be with you.

My mind tries,
to translate the birdsong fights.
Hopes to find new words,
to describe natures worlds.

But...

Till the sun dies
and the sea dries,
my mind will think of you.
Till the moon dives
and the night lights,
my heart will be with you.

My mind wants,
to fly away longs.
In solitude creates
a universe of open gates.

But. . .

Till the sun dies
and the sea dries,
till the moon dives
and the night lights,
I will be in love with you.

A LOVE

I am gonna send you my heart in a dream.
Don't be mean.
I will send you my mind to read.
Don't weep.
I am gonna send you a love just for you.
Please be true.
I will send you a kiss for goodnight.
Stay the night.

Starry day, take me away.
Make me fly to my guy.
Moonless night, search for my knight.
He is the one, i am no longer alone.

My dreams have stolen me from life.
My love for you reaches the afterlife.
I will love you till death and more.
Come on give me a kiss and close your hearts' door.

Can we have a word?
Can we have a love?
Can we be a we?
Can you be one with me?

CHIMERA

I am chasing a chimera the whole of my life,
trying to be good, thoughtful and nice.
I am chasing a chimera trying to love you.
What a dreadful obligation that life needs two.

It is only an utopia to believe in love,
when hate is what makes the world move on.
Hate for anothers' success, makes us
successful, only to be in a state of fuss.

Chimera is believing in peace and unity,
when one sees to another just an opportunity,
to be in a much higher place,
to find his immaculate grace.

Chimera is loving you and your soul,
when all you did is that you stole,
my innocence and my good heart.
Me and love must live apart.

HARD TIMES

I don't need my heart anymore,
i don't need the pain she gives me.
Wish i could find the door,
which will take me away from me.

I don't need myself anymore.
I don't need the mess she gives me.
Me and her have lost the core
and how i wish i could just be.

Without emotions, thoughts and tears.
Without the dragon that have become my fears.
Being without self and heart,
would be a new kind of living art.

I don't need me anymore.
We have reached a dead end.
What to cry for, what to live for?
When you don't have yourself as a friend?

THINKER

I believe that there are powers unknown.
I believe in trees which live on their own.
I believe in ants that strive for food.
I believe that God has left us for good.

My mind searches for new feelings,
my heart is ready for new healings.
A gap marks that i am growing old,
and i am writing my new story in bold.

Away from thoughts that gave me nothing,
away from friends that stole me something.
I am in need for a new fidelity
and i turn my eyes to things that have eternity.

Like sea, trees, mountains, moon,
like love, family, poetry and myths.
I want to be somebody else soon,
I want nature to give me all her gifts.

DREAMS

I must change my eyes, to see where God lives.
Is it sea, moon, trees or sky?
No, it is in my dreams where God lives,
telling me the truth with no lie.

Stop the sun from coming out,
stop the moon from falling down.
Slowly i am breathing, i want to hear my soul shout,
this life has treated me as a clown.

Only in my dreams i can be me,
living lives that my eyes have never see.
Only in my dreams i can be free,
free to be even a mighty tree.

Are dreams scenes of lives past
or from future lives that will last?
I am scared cause only nightmares i see.
Don't want in another endless fear to be.

NOW

Now you see me, now you don't.
I don't care if you say i am not,
the cool girl you will love to love a lot.
All i know is that in my net you are caught.

Now you feel me, now you don't.
You are just my minds' knot.
Although you say i am what you sought,
your eyes lie and that's not my thought.

Now you need me, now you don't.
You must know you are not my want.
I always for liberty fought
and you are just another fault.

Now you hear me, now you don't.
You did all and everything wrong.
Now you want me, now you don't.
I don't care, alone i am not. . .

I've got myself to live for,
i've got myself to fight for,
i've got myself to smile for.
I've got myself to love.

CRY

Cry the tears i have cried for you,
now you are back and you say you are new.
Fear the fears i have feared from you
and you will be trembling, that is true.

Cry my tears and you will understand
that under the same sky we all stand.
We all are equal, women and men,
we all cry, we all love, if we can.

Cry your tears, do not be shy,
let God, do not ask Him why.
Why we are all truly alone,
why all the Love has gone.

Cry the tears, that bring us together,
tears of happiness, will last forever.
When everything and all will end,
i will always remember you as my friend.

A DATE

In solitude i found my mood,
being alone sometimes is good.
Fearful i was for being lonely
but now my time is for me only.

In my mind is a great place to be,
having dreams you can see,
like watching a film in private.
It is like having with yourself a date.

FOR YOU.

Remember the times we used to have together.
Seemed that life could be like that forever.
Now you leave me for someone else
and my whole life, like snow, melts.

I had to break you with my heart,
i had to kill you with my kiss.
I had to feel you to be smart,
i had to steal you to find bliss.

If only i knew how i would be without you,
i would have forgiven you more.
I would have chosen the door,
that leads straight to the core of you.

Now i am all alone banging my head to the wall.
Now i am all with me and i am having my great fall.
If love is this fire that burns my soul,
with you i know i could have it all.

LOVE ATTACK

For me my life is your mind.
I am bewitched by you and i leave behind
myself, before my heart grows old.
Let us meet in a dream and be bold.

As shadows play in front of my window,
i see your face even in my pillow.
Can love exist as opposites attract
or will you be another scar in my heart?

I hug the sun and kiss the moon.
It is January and i feel it is June.
Your love attack brings me back
to my youth, when i could feel truth.

Unmarried i will stay for your sake,
you are my powerful heartache.
If love had a face, it would be yours.
I am giving up all my wars.

MIND THE MIND

Never mind, things change,
feelings and thoughts travel so fast. Mind the mind, be strange,
before you become a forgotten past.

Mind the gap between you and others,
having an ego always bothers.
Be the wind that kisses flowers,
be a man with exquisite powers.

Be yourself when all odds are against you,
find the strength to be your rescue.
Mind the mind when rain falls,
don't accept anything false.

Like the night meet your sunny day,
like a star find your sky and stay.
Believe you have a mighty soul,
mind the head, this is your goal.

FANTASY

Does my fantasy bothers you?
You know, fantasy is where i grew.
Inside her l have built my home,
i have found a friend, i am not alone.

Fantasy is like a land inside me.
There i can be totally free.
There you and me are in love.
I have even met our Lord above.

She is my mechanism of defense,
there the unbeliavable makes sense.
Inside her my dreams come true.
In fantasy i always want to break through.

I have two minds that work for me.
My mind and fantasy make me be,
a powerful human with sensitivity.
Fantasy, you know, takes ability.

SILENCE

Your silence makes my heart bleed,
you are the person i am in need.
I am afraid to hear my tears.
To touch my heart, my heart fears.

My eyes can't see you and they hurt.
Your voice only in memories is heard.
Father, only in photographs i can look for you.
How to live without you, i have no clue.

Life has a tormentous end,
leaving behind lives that can't be mend.
What is the meaning of death,
i think about it with every breath.

Only grave silence remains
and memories tight me like chains.
I have an inner voice that speaks to you,
waiting for my death, the only thing to do.

TOGETHER ALONE

Searching for love, when all alone,
looking at the past, where we seemed we could last.
Searching for love, when all alone,
feeling just without you, even when I am with you.

Together and alone, where all the love has gone,
looking just inside me, only to remind me,
that loving you meant, loosing myself,
when all you ever loved, was only yourself.

I am asking you why, your answer is goodbye.
I try to do my best, you like all the rest.
I try to be your home, you want to be alone.
I only live to love you, you only live to love you.

HOW CAN

When me becomes we,
how can I be me again.
When be is not to be,
how can I be again.

When we are not a we,
how can we be we again.
When me loses me,
how can I be me again.

How can I be me again,
how can we be we again,
how can I be you again,
how can. . .when I can't. . .
meet my destiny. . .meet my destiny.
How can I. . .meet my destiny.

TODAY

Rainy day today,
summer lost its way.
Clouds cry, winds not shy,
raindrops fly.
The drums in the sky,
play a rocky lullaby.
Nature awakens and
i am smelling grass essence.
Black turned the day,
summer far away.

ME AND YOU

You are not just you,
you are not just my love,
you are not just my smile,
you are not just my heart.

You are my love
and love is you.
So do me the honor
and say the I do.

You are the one I want to see,
when I am feeling down, when I can't be me.
You are the one, I truly miss,
when I go to sleep, with your goodnight kiss.

When I found you, I did find me
and together as we, we can truly be free.
When I found you, I had only me
but then as we, I find the reason to be.

You are not just you,
you are me and you.
That's what you are,
me and you.
You are my love
and love is you.
So do me the honor
and say the I do.

I AM

Mistake after mistake
and fear after fear,
the time I was to make
was the time I did the break.

Mistake after mistake
and guilt after guilt,
the heart I had to give
was the heart that couldn't forgive.

And I am. . .Saying just to say, praying just to pray,
crying just to cry, living just to lie.

Crying for all the lying, and crying feels like dying.
Alone to find my home, alone to find my soul.

When reason has no reason and sense is out of sense,
then tears which have no words, say the strongest words.

And I am. . .Saying just to say, praying just to pray,
crying just to cry, living just to lie.

Mistake after mistake
and day after day,
I am just all the same,
when I've lost shame.

Mistake after mistake
and tonight as every night.
Dreaming to forget
the life I had to make.

YOU

Want what you want,
I just want to be with you.
Want what you want,
I just want to live with you.

Look in my eyes and you will only see you.
Sleep in my hands and you will feel my heart names you.
Feel my own silence and you can hear me calling you.
Be in mind and you will know I only think of you.

You, only you, that's the me I want to be.
You, only you, that's the one I want to see.
You, only you, that's the life I want to do.
You, only you, you are my love, my only true.

ME, MYSELF AND I

The mirror is asking why, to be yourself you are shy.
The eyes start to cry, what the feelings want to hide.
The why is standing by, while life is flying by
and friends tell no lie, when friendship says goodbye.

Me, myself and I, asking a silent why.
Me, myself and I, searching in the cry,
why me, myself and I are trying to deny,
that me, myself and I are living just to die.

Living just to lie, living just to cry,
living to deny, me, myself and I.
Living just to die, that's why.

The nights come to hide, that my dreams have no life.
The day becomes today, a today like yesterday.
Having winter although May, having nothing more to say,
having no other way, but being just an empty day. . .

ADVICE

Pick your battles, count your blessings,
all these advice, oh, so depressing.
Let my mind think, out of your thoughts.
Let me solve the puzzle of my minds knots.

Fighting to be me in a world so friendly,
everyone with an opinion that comes out gently.
On how to live life, on how to be me.
Oh, how i wish i could be lost at sea.

Make me forget my own will,
make me pay their own bill.
Alone and thinking i'd rather be,
than in a lost of self loving we.

Pick your battles, count your blessings,
in a world where everybody are kings
on their fellow life, let me be as stubborn
as i want. I have myself to govern.

WHY

I can blame my age, for wanting to change the page
or maybe it's the Spring, which made your heart spring.

We can have the fight, which will last all night,
we can talk the fears, and can scream our
tears. . .

You can blame me and I can blame you,
but it's only true, that goodbye takes two.
Let's finally agree our last words to be,
I loved you and you loved me.

Don't ask me why, I don't have any tears left to cry.
It would only be a sad, sad lie, to say goodbye,
when nothing good I can find in our bye.

HUMAN

I don't know, maybe it's my imagination,
maybe i must blame my destination,
but i still can't find my way
and it's hard enough to get it through the day.

It seems like in the society of angels,
i am the only devil.
Like a black sheep among white,
i am gonna start a fight
between good and evil.

If good is the heart and evil the mind,
this is a machine soul that can only rewind
the past·no present,no future
for this human who can't be mature.

What can i choose for this life?
Mind, heart, body or soul?
They are all inside me in a fight
and i am the one standing like a fool.

In the society of angels, i am the only devil.
Doing harm to myself is my evil.
Depriving myself from my future
is my convicting failure.

What can i do?
Heart crying, mind missing.
Body needing, soul searching.
And me. . .forgetting me.

What is the problem with me?
I do not love me.
Cause i am not what i wanted to be
and i am all alone in a life called sea.

Betrayed from myself
i am like a silence among tears
and i can't help myself
to escape from the horrible fears.

Less words are always more.
Losing the essence, losing the core.
I don't know, mind can't think,
maybe i would be better off if i was a thing.

Why am i writing all these?
Cause we are all and an angel and a demon.
In a world where mind has seized
all powers, how i wish i was a lonely lemon.

ROTTEN ROYALS

My body is my castle but my soldiers
are away, leaving me completely defenceless.
I am away from myself for a long time now
and i am searching for someone-me-to blame.

Rotten royals are my mind and heart,
once the jewellery of my crown.
Rotten royals that betray me every day.
Bitter enemies against their body that is their land.

Having the enemy inside you, with
the key lost in a far away place.
There is no hope for survival, there
is no light at the end of the tunel.

I have as enemies my heart and mind,
those remembering that once were young
and beautiful. Now old and ugly
they give me the worse tears of my life.

MEMORY

In the centuries to come life will live on
and we will all be memories, if so.
I am standing like a future memory in front of you
and i want to make my remembrance.

I am not as sunny as the sun,
i am more heavy, like rain in a stormy evening.
I am more like clouds with no story
and like a tree with no fruits.

The memory of me will soon fade away,
as i have no children to remember me.
Only my writings will stand like a statue,
like a proof of me passing from life.

Tears in my eyes remind me, that my soul is a river
and for mind i have the wind.
As for my heart, she can't stop bleeding
and my body has its roots in liberty.

Can all these make me a memory?

BLUE

Sea inside, tear outside,
black inside, white outside,
mad inside, calm outside,
crying inside, smiling outside.

My everyday way, just my every day.
When they ask me how do you do,
I simply say, fine how are you.
But that's not at all, oh no, not at all true,
cause I always feel blue.

And when I am blue, I think of you,
when I am blue, I dream of you
and when I am blue, I only want,
just to be with you.

Cause with you I can be
just as simple as a tree,
just as free as the sea,
just as starry as the sky,
yes with you I can be,
I can be so free of me.

Oh, how I wish I could be
a simple, simple happy me.
How I wish I could be,
I could be so free of me.

Heart inside, mind outside,
child inside, man outside,
strange inside, strangers outside
night inside, day outside.
My everyday way, just my every day.

How do you do?
I do blue. . .that's how I do. . .blue. . ..

NEW AGE

Out of internet, out of communication
Find life in the new application.
In silence we meet, in silence we understand,
in a fantasy world now i stand.

Alien and analphabet,
not knowing how to use the net.
New age, new words,
a whole universe of worlds.

Platforms and codes the new homes,
pseudonyms and avatars the new names.
The lights of the screen enlighten the mind,
outside life runs, oh never mind.

Digital solitude, reach out for me.
We all live in a digital sea.
Do not be lost in the crowd,
new generation, write out loud.

Write in your phone, tablet or PC,
find the new way to be.
Watch out for the virus, the new disease,
oh Lord, make internet never cease.

A SMALL HAPPINESS

Free is my mind when he is blind
to things around me that bind me.
I am leaving behind my past,
maybe my present will last.

I am feeling a small happiness,
as i am in a state of loneliness.
Just feeling my mind thinking,
just feeling my heart beating.

It is in silence where i can find me,
in solitude where i can be really me.
Other people don't understand me,
other people make me feel a stranger to me.

Maybe i must pass this lonely period,
to stop feeling like an idiot.
When all around me there is noise,
my mind my happiness destroys.

NOT IN LOVE

I am having third thoughts on you,
don't know if you are truly true.
What to compare with the sea
of feelings i have inside of me?

Nothing can answer to my why,
why our love must say goodbye.
But you are not in love with me,
although you say we could be a we.

I am like a desert waiting to be an oasis,
but our hearts will be in different places.

DREAM

Dream and dream a great bit of me,
dream and you will suddenly see,
my heart standing in front of you.
You know, i always was in fond of you.

Daydream and nightdream would do,
to bring together me and you.
In our minds we always meet,
to dream of you it is so sweet.

Dreams are my rescue.
I escape from life and meet you.
Let's make this dream come true,
let's fall in love me and you.

THE PROPHECY

Did you read the prophecy about the soul,
the journey she makes before the great fall?
Did you hear the prophecy about the heart,
the pains she must go through before she becomes art?

Life is the finest and purest kind of art,
anytime you can finish your plans and again start.
Your mind is a magic machine
and you are in sky and earth between.

The sun searches for the loving moon,
as you live in your graceful balloon.
Love makes your breathing to count in gold,
all the precious moments you write in your mind with bold.

The prophecy is here to be fulfilled,
to make your soul completely thrilled.
The prophecy says be the best of you
and that means simply stay true.

UTOPIA

Melancholy is an utopia,
crisis comes from your egopathy.
Emphasis is given on harmony,
but sarcasm is your parallel method.

Apology comes as an ironic practise,
is it ethical, you say,to have blasphemy as stigma?
Everyone has a dialogue with God,
no dogma can have an antagonism with that.

In a emphatic way you organise your life,
the chaos in your character.
You hypocrite, you are nothing but a demon,
but in your fantasy you live in paradise.

Your epilogue will come from your antagonism,
you will be a protagonist in a scandal.
Your Psyche is a cruel phenomenon,
pure philanthropy writing about your utopia.

LIVE

Life is a narrow bridge full of flowers with thorns.
You can bleed or you can lead.
Don't ask, in what world i am thrown?
Don't shout wrong, fight to be strong.

Suffocating life can be, pain drowns you like the sea.
Death the inescapable cage, life can lead you to outrage.
Life means death, so until your last breath,
stay you and true. Maybe bad but never sad.

The future ahead needs your head
to be clear, with no fear.
That is what father said to his son,
who killed himself because he didn't won. . ..life.

BLACK ROSE

Black rose, my mind blows
to the sight of you, although i am blue.
Nature around me, just to remind me
everything is posing, my heart closing.

Black rose, my mind is prose.
Nobody to hear, nobody near.
My eyes lost in you, yes it is true,
i am all alone, my friends are gone.

Black rose, my tears are close
to my eyes. My love said his goodbyes.
A new life ahead for me, like a sea.
A new way, how i wish i could fly
away.

Black rose, my soul knows
that everything dies, even lies.
Like you, i was once beautiful and true.
Now i am only sad, miserable and bad.

TWICE IN A BLUE MOON

My tears open my heart and more tears come out.
I want to hear my hearts voice, she wants to shout.
Twice in a blue moon, i respect her.
In silence i feel her, i know she is there.

What is the need of the heart, when
all she gives me is unbearable pain?
What is the use of her, when all she
commands me to do is just be?

Twice in a blue moon, i search her truth.
She often cries about her youth.
Twice in a blue moon, i give her a hug,
but most often i have her as a rug.

My mind walks on her with indifference,
my body uses her with no defense.
I leave her alone, crying in the dark.
My heart is my secret, deep, bleeding mark.

MY CHRISTMAS

My Christmas is blue,
i am missing you.
My Christmas is white,
we had our last fight.

I will remember this December,
with my tears and my fears.
I will remember this December,
as the only December through the years.

This time of year i always cry,
you went away without a why.
This time of year i am all alone,
you went away and all my love has gone.

My Christmas is blue,
i think of you.
My Christmas in my mind,
is my tears that made me blind.

My Christmas is blue.
My Christmas is you.

COLORFUL CHRISTMAS

Christmas is white,
let us stop the fight.
Let us make tonight,
our life to shine bright.

Christmas is red,
Santa has read,
our wishes are heard
and love in the world is spread.

Christmas is blue,
i am kissing you.
Make my heart true,
you know love needs two.

Christmas is green,
i am wearing my jean.
I feel like a queen.
Let us stop being mean.

Christmas is love,
let us reach the above
and send Him a dove,
to the One that is Love.

FREEDOM

I am free to be free but i am caged,
by thoughts, surroundings and emotions.
My soul with myself outraged
and i am afraid of mind explotions.

What is freedom when you are free?
Not even an idea, a wanting, a feeling.
Urgent in a relationship to be
and work until your head has a ceiling.

Are we truly free when we die
or do we come back again to be alive?
Are we truly free or is it a minds lie,
being under the urge to survive?

Freedom for everyone on earth is a need.
For freedom hearts, bodies and minds have bleed.
But when you are free, respect this gift.
This is a situation that can quickly shift.

MY STYLE

You me. . .perfect we. . .
making today, feel like the day
for which hearts pray
and words have nothing to say.

You me. . .perfect we. . .
smile to smile. . .time to time
word to word. . .eye to eye,
can you be, my only one.

You me. . .perfect we. . .
You me. . .in harmony.

Maybe it's your eyes, maybe it's your lies,
maybe it's your looks or maybe it's your books.
Maybe it's your voice or maybe you are my choice,
maybe it's your style, but baby, I don't care,
cause you are my style. . .

You me. . .perfect we. . .

MY FRIEND

You are the friend, I want to defend.
You are the friend, I can depend.
You are the friend, I have no pretend.
You are my friend and friends have no end.

Oh dear friend, please don't cry
when all of your questions, lead to a why.
Sun will set and sun will rise,
day will follow after the night.

Oh dear friend, please don't cry
say your goodbyes, before the journey high.
Life is a child, who wants to fly,
to live in the clouds, to live in the sky.

Oh dear friend, please don't cry
the reason we live is to happily die.
Oh dear friend, please don't cry
the reason we die is to live in the sky.

You are the friend, I would recommend.
You are the friend, I would never lend.
You are the friend, where feelings are meant.
You are my friend and our love has no end.

FACE

The lines of my face give me a new route.
I must deeply respect their truth.
They come from years of joy and tears,
they count my lifes' loving and fears.

I can't look my face with a smile,
i am guilty of being heart hostile.
My face tells the truth i want to hide,
that i am all alone and nobodys' bride.

If face is the mirror of the soul,
i see that my soul has a hole.
Thoughts and emotions in my eyes,
locked inside me even when my face cries.

How much i owe to my face i don't know
but i know i want it to glow.
From happiness and love undenied,
then i will find all of its lines right.

MAKE LOVE

My heart depends on you.
I can her telling me this is true.
Oh, the sky such a surprise.
To touch the clouds in your green eyes.

Stars are crying tonight,
jealous of our loving light.
Fragile roses smell like you
and your mind my endless view.

I only make love never do sex.
Never had love as a night guest.
I love you, can you hear?
When with you, LORD is here.

Mountains around me, just your arms.
With every kiss, Spring comes.
Dancing lights, moon and sea,
love, oh love, sleep with me.

THE DIVORCE

Liar, liar you are my fire.
You burned my dreams down
and you made me feel like a clown.
Liar, liar, oh you, my false desire.

Blind is the freedom of my heart.
You made me feel oh so bad.
You said we'd never be apart
but now all i know is how to be sad.

Dreams take me away tonight,
travel me to where i can be the sunlight.
Rain do not make me live my life in vain,
cause i have finished the school of pain.

Love you are now my enemy.
Feeling you would be heavenly
but without you i can be me,
living my existence all so free.

JUST BREATHING

Everything annoys me, even
the sound of me breathing.
I think i would hate heaven
this rainy, unhearted evening.

Lightings come as a reminder
that every moment times change.
But i am getting blinder and blinder
and my mind thinks so strange.

Wanting to be free of thinking,
wanting to be free of feeling.
Can i cry a rain to be believed
or must i shout a thunder to be pleased?

This rainy, unhearted evening
i understood i have lost my soul.
There is no such thing as reasoning,
when you don't know what is your role.

DAY

Day after day,
i prayed for you to stay.
In the midst of May,
Winter came my way. . .
You went away.

You found my heart to play
and my tears dare say,
a coward must pay,
for pure hearts that pray.

You are my groundhog day.
I was just your April fools day.

REBORN

My Psyche dies within me from melancholy.
To be in hate with God, is it unholy?
I long the day i will die.
Do not want to be reborn and that's no lie.

My eyes lost in the sculptured cloud.
My body bound to be fertile ground.
My beauty has the dreadful duty,
to old me ugly, that's natures cruelty.

How many lives must i live before i really die?
How many souls must i change before the brave goodbye?
From this circle of life i want to be free.
Living once was enough for me.

Reborn as though unborn,
with no memory of the past century,
is like a prison with no reason,
is like judging with no justice.

Being tormented, is it now enough?
Unloved life to live is tough.
Where is my salvation?
Liberty has forgotten my generation.

Oh LORD, there is no hope.

BABEL

We all live in a sentimental Babel
and it will be quite late when He will ring the bell,
to make our hearts clear, to be real.
Oh people, now it is the time to feel.

To feel our sense and mind, to feel
our loved ones, to be kind and heal
all our pains. Here is the time to seal
our fears and see things clear.

Babel is the name of the mind,
when to reality it is blind.
Babel is the name of the soul,
when she has forgotten her role.

The time is now to prove our rights,
to give our soul to the good fights.
For health, freedom and bread,
our hearts and minds must be heard.

SAY YOU DO

Do you want to walk hand in hand,
do you want to run just for fun,
do you feel like dancing in the street,
do you want to sleep with my heartbeat.

Say you do, you do, you do
cause I truly love you.
Yes I do, I do, I do
and I want to live with you.

I don't have anything, although I have everything,
if I don't have you, you must say the I do,
cause I truly, truly, truly love you,
yes I do, I do, I do, I do truly love you.

Do you want to have my name,
do you feel we are the same.
Do you find in me your reason to be,
do you want to live with me.

Say you do, you do, you do,
cause I truly love you.
Yes I do, I do, I do,
and I want to live with you. . .

WHEN MINDS FLY

Giving someone the cold shoulder,
when his mind flies away,
when with his words speaks louder,
will cause a painful payday.

His voice will become stronger,
no indifference will be accepted any longer.
His dreams will wear a poetry face
and all mistake his voice will erase.

When pigs fly, he will stop writing,
all obstacles seem so inviting.
A blessing in disguise the negatives,
he only counts his prerogatives.

When minds fly, give them wings,
with your good words and your blessings.
When minds fly, hear their music,
being a poet always needs musing.

AWAY

You say, you'll love me all the way,
that I am your perfect day,
you think my smile is May,
you pray I am here to stay...you say...

You say, that love is the only way,
that life is not a play...
You say, that there'll come a day,
when leaving you will say, I gave your heart
away...but

Away, is the only way, just to find my way,
let us stay away, till I am all OK.
Oh no, I have nothing more to say,
I have no need to pray, just let me stay away...
until I find my way...let me be...my way.

You say, that I am your perfect day,
I am a kind of May...
You say, my love is your horey,
like dying will be our away...but...

DESTINY

Is my destiny Gods' will
or will my actions make the final bill?
Is it my destiny to be all alone
or am i living in a twilight zone?

Destiny is our story waiting to be written
and nothing in our way is forbidden.
Mind and heart is our machine,
that play our film in our private screen.

Chance and luck are hiding from us,
playing with us and making a fuss.
A tunel is life, the light is there
and we must only live and dare.

Destiny will be our perfect book,
having our own, on life, private look.
Destiny will be the answer to God,
for what we gave our soul, for what we fought.

SORROW

How many flies have we killed?
How many animals were our meal?
How many sins can God count
In this soul i carry as my wound?

Some say, for what to live if you are a fly?
Do they love, laugh or cry?
Or others say, for what to live if you are a snake?
Do they hug, regret or create?

Nature for me is a mystery,
been like that throughout history.
But animals life shouldn't be a bother,
they too have a mother.

How many of my tears
were for animals i do not know.
But i know i have fears,
If i come back as an animal what will i do?

I do not want to be killed to be a meal,
or to pain in vain with nobody to care for me.
What is the use of having a voice,
when you do not have a real choice?

I feel regret and sorrow,
there must be another path to follow.
Deep in my heart i am sorry.
What animals have to do with human glory?

THE ENEMY

Don't think and feel any further,
the enemy you seek is inside you.
Stand in front of the mirror like a man not a feather
and you will see the enemy in front of you.

You will kill him by killing your eyes,
the ones that see you and despise.
You will kill him by killing your heart,
the one that makes you feel like a coward.

The enemy is being the less of you,
the fear of losing the whole of you.
The enemy is only your bad self,
must he disappear after twelve.

Like in a fairytale be the hero,
which will turn your monster to a zero.
Find inside you the strength to be you
and you will see that dreams come true.

OUT OF ORDER

Out of job, out of hope,
nothing left to me but God.
In a world where all around us is money,
i am like a bee with no honey.

Out of order, with no order.
Life grows me to be older
and soon there will be no use of me.
Age beats me with such cruelty.

I am in the need for a loan,
but i know they wouldn't give me one.
I am in the need for love,
but i am left penniless and alone.

All i need is a simple job.
I don't think i ask a lot.
But today jobs are like gold·
those who have them, those they hold.

I do not even have the basics.
Food, rent, clothes, only bills.
I must finally accept and face this:
i am a useless human of wills.

OUT OF FAITH

I know it by heart the poem i must say but i will not say it.
I know it by the book what i must do
but i will not do it.

My mind is a new horizon of freedom.
My heart is in need of a new kingdom.

All i see around me make me look inside, by fear
and i do not want anyone who knows it all to come near.

My fidelity broken, nobody to hear.
My hopes from the sky disappear.
I am a woman out of trust and faith
and i am waiting the results of wrath.

Can fear make me be good?
Or is this question too rude?
I don't see God nowhere else
but nature and there jungle prevails.
I only see us in our cells
saying thank you for the good days.

Am i too bad or as they say
without God we'll be mad.
Can't think of a better time to reinvent sky and earth,
with love giving birth to a new God,
more humane and zoophilous,
more close to what i can call LORD.

FALLING

I kiss the morning good night.
Didn't sleep tonight.
I have been waiting for my knight
and everything seems right.

I am falling in love with you,
i can't believe this is true.
I am falling out of my past,
wishing our love will last.

I am falling in your arms
and my heart plays the drums.
I am falling for your heart.
Come on,let the magic start.

You and me, like moon and sea.
Dancing lights in the nights.
You and me, falling angels we,
making love feel that miracles are real.

GARDEN

Trees around me speak so loud,
sunny rain and dancing cloud.
My fingertips touch the flower land.
Inside the miracle of nature i stand.

Oh, my garden, such a museum,
living statues dancing with the wind.
Roses, dandelions, fairies and lillium
palm and orange trees, pines all so kind.

Although like statues they stand,
they've got soul inside.
And in this colorful land,
i see that nature has an archaeological side.

FLOWERS

I play music for my flowers.
I believe they have secret powers,
to heal, to make us feel
that good in this world is real.

As the sun rays rest upon them,
i know i am looking at natures' gem.
Magic in my eyes, which tell no lies.
Nature in my mind, has no failure.

A moment i spend looking at my flowers
but their memory stays with me for hours.
Wish i was so care free, feeding the hungry bee.
Wish i was so useful and always youthful.

I play music for my flowers.
I think they are lonely.
If only i could have God powers.
This world would be for flowers only.

NATURE

Birds fight for bread, being out of breath.
Ants search for food, doing their everyday route.
Cicadas sing, till they lose the last fragment of being.
Fish are hungry, being with the sea very angry.

All around me death and life,
how i wish i could cut injustice with a knife.
All around me Gods works,
but i am wondering how He works.

Leaving his creatures die for life,
all alone in a cruel, cruel world.
They all for food and home strive,
they all die with an unanswered why.

Why they are born, as if thrown,
in a world where their existence,
is as though a burden, a clown
for some, a death sentence.

Known to all but unspoken,
we are all guilty for the forgotten.
We have lost our animals nature,
and we are unhuman towards other creature.

FRAGMENTS OF AFTERLIFE

Possible even the impossible
and in the underworld there is life.
I am standing in the gates of Hades,
only human alive among the dead.

Voices scream, chanting i am an Angel
and all around dead but still alive Demons.
I am walking in the darkness,
is this where souls end up?
I am afraid to breath, letting others know i am the alive here.

I have no words to describe the unspoken,
the horrible smell, the dirty waters, the cold down there.
But most of all the animal situation of the humans.
Left all alone, with wounds in their bodies, killing and living all over again.

Where is God i wondered, leaving Satan do his work?
Million reasons to cry but where can one find tears.
Soulless, humanless, with animals at their best.
I thought afterlife is our punishment for the cruelty we give to animals
and. . .

Then i woke up.

www.ingramcontent.com/pod-product-compliance
Lightning Source LLC
Chambersburg PA
CBHW070702100426
42735CB00039B/2442